Let's Read About Our Bodies
Conozcamos nuestro cuerpo

Ear/Orejas

Cynthia Klingel & Robert B. Noyed
photographs by/fotografías por Gregg Andersen

Reading consultant/Consultora de lectura: Cecilia Minden-Cupp, Ph.D.,
Adjunct Professor, College of Continuing and Professional Studies, University of Virginia

Weekly Reader.
EARLY LEARNING LIBRARY

For a free color catalog describing Weekly Reader® Early Learning Library's list of high-quality books, call 1-877-445-5824 or fax your request to (414) 336-0164.

Library of Congress Cataloging-in-Publication Data

Klingel, Cynthia.
    Ears = Orejas / by Cynthia Klingel and Robert B. Noyed. — [Bilingual ed.]
      p. cm. — (Let's read about our bodies = Conozcamos nuestro cuerpo)
    Includes bibliographical references and index.
    Summary: A bilingual introduction to ears, what they are used for, and how to take care of them.
    ISBN 0-8368-3071-7 (lib. bdg.)
    ISBN 0-8368-3320-1 (softcover)
    1. Ears—Juvenile literature. [1. Ears. 2. Hearing. 3. Senses and sensation. 4. Spanish language materials—Bilingual.] I. Title: Orejas. II. Noyed, Robert B. III. Title.
    QM507.K56   2002
    612.8′5—dc21   2001055090

This edition first published in 2002 by
Weekly Reader® Early Learning Library
330 West Olive Street, Suite 100
Milwaukee, WI 53212 USA

Copyright © 2002 by Weekly Reader® Early Learning Library

An Editorial Directions book
Editors: E. Russell Primm and Emily Dolbear
Translators: Tatiana Acosta and Guillermo Gutiérrez
Art direction, design, and page production: The Design Lab
Photographer: Gregg Andersen
Weekly Reader® Early Learning Library art direction: Tammy Gruenewald
Weekly Reader® Early Learning Library page layout: Katherine A. Goedheer

Printed in the United States of America

2 3 4 5 6 7 8 9 06 05 04 03 02

Note to Educators and Parents

As a Reading Specialist I know that books for young children should engage their interest, impart useful information, and motivate them to want to learn more.

Let's Read About Our Bodies is a new series of books designed to help children understand the value of good health and of taking care of their bodies.

A young child's active mind is engaged by the carefully chosen subjects. The imaginative text works to build young vocabularies. The short, repetitive sentences help children stay focused as they develop their own relationship with reading. The bright, colorful photographs of children enjoying good health habits complement the text with their simplicity to both entertain and encourage young children to want to learn – and read – more.

These books are designed to be used by adults as "read-to" books to share with children to encourage early literacy in the home, school, and library. They are also suitable for more advanced young readers to enjoy on their own.

Una nota a los educadores y a los padres

Como especialista en lectura, sé que los libros infantiles deben interesar a los niños, proporcionar información útil y motivarlos a aprender.

Conozcamos nuestro cuerpo es una nueva serie de libros pensada para ayudar a los niños a entender la importancia de la salud y del cuidado del cuerpo.

Los temas, cuidadosamente seleccionados, mantienen ocupada la activa mente del niño. El texto, lleno de imaginación, facilita el enriquecimiento del vocabulario infantil. Las oraciones, breves y repetitivas, ayudan a los ninos a centrarse en la actividad mientras desarrollan su propia relación con la lectura. Las bellas fotografías de niños que disfrutan de buenos hábitos de salud complementan el texto con su sencillez, y consiguen entretener a los niños y animarlos a aprender nuevos conceptos y a leer más.

Estos libros están pensados para que los adultos se los lean a los niños, con el fin de fomentar la lectura incipiente en el hogar, en la escuela y en la biblioteca. También son adecuados para que los jóvenes lectores más avanzados los disfruten leyéndolos por su cuenta.

Cecilia Minden-Cupp, Ph.D., Adjunct Professor,
College of Continuing and Professional Studies, University of Virginia

These are my ears.
I have two ears.

- - - - - - -

Éstas son mis orejas.
Tengo dos orejas.

I have an ear on
each side of my head.

- - - - - - -

Tengo una oreja en
cada lado de la cabeza.

I use my ears to hear.

- - - - - - -

Uso las orejas para oír.

I can use my ears
to listen to songs.

- - - - - - -

Puedo usar las orejas
para escuchar canciones.

I can use my ears to listen to my friends.

- - - - - - - -

Puedo usar las orejas para escuchar a mis amigos.

I take good care of
my ears. I never put
anything in my ears!

– – – – – – –

Me cuido muy bien las
orejas. ¡Nunca me meto
nada en las orejas!

I cover my ears
when noises are loud.

Me tapo las orejas
cuando los ruidos
son fuertes.

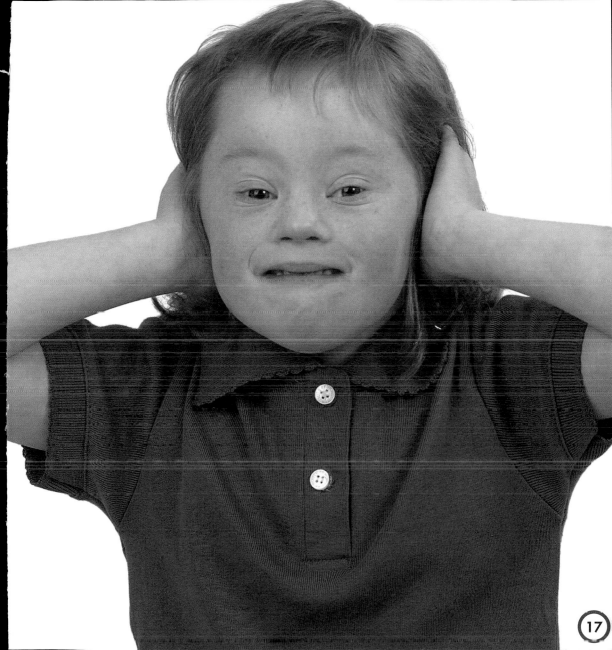

I cover my ears with
a hat when it is cold.

Me tapo las orejas
con un gorro cuando
hace frío.

Shhhh! Listen.
What can you hear?

– – – – – – –

¡Chisss! Escucha.
¿Qué puedes oír?

Glossary/Glosario

hear–to sense sounds with the ear
oír–percibir sonidos con el oído

listen–to pay attention in order to hear
escuchar–prestar atención para oír algo

noises–sounds
ruidos–sonidos

For More Information/Más información

Fiction Books/Libros de ficción
Dooley, Virginia. *Tubes in My Ears: My Trip to the Hospital.*
　New York: Mondo, 1996.
Perkins, Al. *The Ear Book.* New York: Random House, 1968.

Nonfiction Books/Libros de no ficción
Pringle, Laurence. *Hearing.* Tarrytown, N.Y.: Benchmark
　Books, 2000.
Trumbauer, Lisa. *Animal Ears.* Mankato, Minn.:
　Pebble Books, 2000.

Web Sites/Páginas Web
Let's Hear It for the Ear!
kidshealth.org/kid/body/ear_SW.html
For more information about the different parts of the ear

What Is Earwax?
kidshealth.org/kid/talk/yucky/earwax.html
For information about the purpose of earwax

Index/Índice

About the Authors/Información sobre los autores

Cynthia Klingel has worked as a high school English teacher and an elementary school teacher. She is currently the curriculum director for a Minnesota school district. Cynthia Klingel lives with her family in Mankato, Minnesota.

Cynthia Klingel ha trabajado como maestra de inglés de secundaria y como maestra de primaria. Actualmente es la directora de planes de estudio de un distrito escolar de Minnesota. Cynthia Klingel vive con su familia en Mankato, Minnesota.

Robert B. Noyed started his career as a newspaper reporter. Since then, he has worked in school communications and public relations at the state and national level. Robert B. Noyed lives with his family in Brooklyn Center, Minnesota.

Robert B. Noyed comenzó su carrera como reportero en un periódico. Desde entonces ha trabajado en comunicación escolar y relaciones públicas a nivel estatal y nacional. Robert B. Noyed vive con su familia en Brooklyn Center, Minnesota.